Into the Weeds

JUDITH BUFFALOE
LINDA FAIR
GAIA MIKA

Published by
Into the Weeds Press
Taos, New Mexico
jbuffaloe@gmail.com

Print ISBN:
979-8370044526

Front Cover art by Linda Kemper Fair
Group photo by Rob Stout

We offer these poems in gratitude to the earth and all her children: to the wolf and to the wild onion, to white rhinos, red cliffs and round soft bellies, to all those who nourish our hearts with beauty and wildness. And, finally, to the weeds for keeping us humble and teaching us to never stop growing.

Table of Contents

GAIA MIKA

INTRODUCTION

We are three women joined by 20 years of writing poetry together—which has meant sharing our lives and deepening friendships. Each of us came from different parts of the country to the wild beauty of New Mexico, part of the tradition of women "who rode away" seeking a rougher, freer life.

We found connection through our shared amazement at the inconceivable beauty and mystery of the world of plants and critters, of the vastness of New Mexico skies, and through our shared grief and outrage at what human hubris has wrought.

Each week as we gathered 'round Gaia's table, we offered our words: we laughed, we cried, we raged, and sometimes we were blessed with moments of insight. Once in a while a gem surfaced. The poems you see here have the flavors of all of the above.

Our book's title, *Into the Weeds* reflects our collective and ardently held belief that all of the living world—what we call weeds, pesky insects, and even public figures—asks us to be open and to listen as if our lives depended upon it. And they do.

We invite you to take a walk into the weeds with us now.

JUDITH BUFFALOE.

TWO HORSES IN AN OPEN FIELD

After lightning scoured the air
and the rain had almost stopped
we found two horses
together
where they had fallen
by the pond
their bodies
close to the barbed wire fence.

Their one shape
outlined by burnt grass—
a last leaping moment.

Singed hair ringed
the tops of their hooves
and the hooves coal-black
and shiny as patent slippers
    forged for dancing.

Ask the Skin Horse

I wrote a letter to a real girl today.
She didn't know she was real until she read my letter.
She took the letter to her mother.
See Mother, I am real she said.

Same with a bunny. A rabbit really. Not a real rabbit.
A Velveteen Rabbit embarrassed about his hind legs.
Why don't my legs work like real rabbits?

In other days when everything was real, a friend
and I sat outside the student dining hall to see the moon's eclipse.

Of that eclipse, I remember nothing. I remember our conversation
though, where he posed a question that has followed me since.

What if these dandelions, this blanket,
everything exists only in our imagination.

Like memory? I may have said.   *No, memories are real.*

Like a dream then? Maybe like a dream.

What is real?
    The Skin Horse always tells the truth.
    Ask the Skin Horse.

COURAGE OF THE FENNEL

The poem that wanted to write itself
not the poem I sought
but this poem came in clusters like heads of dill
in a half-dead garden.

Or like fennel drooping beyond extraordinary
measures of resuscitation though still
holding a few proud spokes here and there
and this courage spoke asking to have her seeds,
those barely hanging on the radials of brown
and honey umbrella stalks, asking to have them *seen.*

The poem I meant to write came up
with the new moon, with last day's light
on gold petals of cottonwoods when I stood
alone and knew nothing had been or could be
more than this, acknowledging *this* could
          not be measured.

In the ash tree, starlings bicker as to who has the right
to occupy what, unaware of Ruby the cat
still as a leopard waiting for dark. Myself,
I watch the collected panorama. I formulate
how I could encompass the poem I want to write.
It would write itself I decide, without words,
a flag that says nothing decipherable, incorporates
all that cannot be spoken.

A great I AM for this blink of evening
October's bursting foliage, for brown
fennel's drooping spokes.

RESURRECTION

We still have the fatigues
stored in a box in the root cellar.

Maybe they are the pair you wore
the day you watched Chinese mortars
skip like pebbles across a pond inevitable

    whining

and when the one for you came and found you
in the shallow trench it said *This is yours.*
It said *Give me everything.*

Your chest exploded into brilliant
clumps of earth like honeybees
riding a high voltage line.

So you beheld yourself raw
    dazzling, alive.
Resurrected. And the ring in your ears
with you still—a blessing.

WILD MORNING GLORIES

In another life I would be someone who studies

wildflowers, a woman conversant with Latin names

and common names of larkspurs, wild iris, columbines

and meadow flax. I would cherish the smallest nutlets

of *tribulus terrestrus*, and goatheads' beguiling petals.

Each day I would ponder prickly-glaborous

flower heads, speak to each

as I peer at stigmas, styles, pistils

and chant names of pussytoes, whiteflower,

honeysuckle: *my precious my beauties my rosary.*

In a parallel world I am a slender spinster

devoted to an ordered life simple as bindweed.

I study silvery leaves, find purpose in exactitude

of language quivering at slight variations

in milkweed pollens clustered like sisters

among wild grasses.

TABOO

Somewhere I read C. Milosz' account of how he violated a taboo by killing a water snake and how the wound of the violation followed him his whole life. I felt relief to hear his story, that someone of Milosz' stature could have done something that counter, so not-life-affirming. I felt relief because misery loves to share and I have my own story of taboo violation, though until I read Milosz, I hadn't thought to call it a taboo—I just knew what I did lodged so deep I rarely thought about it. Yet the memory inflicted, when I did recall it took a pink bare pain in my heart— what organ holds Regret? Grief? I will tell this story quickly: I killed some babies, mice babies, but babies. I brought a large rock down hard on a nest of newborns I found under a garbage can in the alley. I was young, junior-high, but knew instinctively, deeply, as Milosz had known...I knew.

GALVESTON HURRICANE 1900-2021

A hurricane made landfall in Galveston, Texas on September 9, 1900.
Over 6000 people died.
My grandparents, James and Sarah Maude Hall, survived.

~~~~~~

They recalled water moccasins' black heads above the swirl.
They didn't say much about the rest of it.

They had seen a storm coming. For a day
the ebony horizon moved closer, the air sticky.

"Ma, this is a big one."

From the second story they watched the rains start,
heard winds shriek and roar. That roar.

"We've ridden them out before."

Mouths made words. No sounds;
window panes lost hold, sewage

crept under doorways, carpets sodden.
Hinges let go in a perfume of salt.

> Rains kept coming
> Houses flooded.

About the school teacher, their friend,
they didn't have much to say. She put on a swimsuit
sat on her roof, dangled her feet in water
(under a clear sky the next morning)
Still the water rose. She stretched a swim cap
over her head, gave a wave and lowered herself.

They might have said why she decided to let go
why some let go and others stay.
Really they didn't have much to say. Rains came
houses flooded.

Everything came loose.

CHRIST IN THE DESERT MONASTERY

Abiquiu, New Mexico

Here for silence I sit in a rocking chair.
It holds me all day without complaint.
I watch hops grow against red cliffs
soaked in rolling sky, naked rocks
and blue-black dazzled magpie feathers.
I talk little, breathe a delicate portion
of fiery gratitude for something
barely heard, something lamentable
high-pitched bells or men's voices
layered through centuries.

I hear the offer of rest.
Irresistible the offer.
Come unto me
I will give you rest.

BOA CONSTRICTOR

My grandmother's braid
resided in the top drawer
of her vanity.

She let me take it out
and hold it
like a friendly boa constrictor.

Was this really yours
I asked her each time
trying to square the old woman
with the fertile vibrancy
of the young woman
whose thick red braid
it had been.

How could she be?
One and the same
copper-headed flowering girl
and dried-up beloved.

My Father Ordinaire

We cannot grow up until we can see our parents as other people.
—C. Jung

Remember   I seek objectivity.   I don't claim it.

Fairy tales and Bible stories provide templates.

Mine is the myth of Jonah.

He ran from his job. He hid on a boat.

　　　He landed in a stormy sea.

Jonah on the lam. Jonah hides from God

Jonah, swallowed by strangeness.

　　　Why me, God?

　　　　　　　*

I have run and grumbled and inflicted headaches
upon myself and now (may this be so)
I hear. I pause. I turn and face... my father.

O Jonah you can run

My father in his commonness. *My Father Ordinaire.*

Late in life I came to a dark wood and I choose to leave warm slippers

to go out and face strangeness

　　　in this luminous pause between mysteries.

A GIRL GOES FORTH

Inspired by Walt Whitman

The girl who became the woman looked at the world
from her mother's breast. The mother's breast became
part of the girl and the breast assured her claim in the world.

The girl became wild sage and long blue throats
of lupine. She became sticky pitch of pine trees' arms.
All are as kin to her as her mother's breast.

Behind her house, the girl discovers sounds
of bawling cows, their waiting-for-slaughter moos
and smells of rendered bodies blending with smells
of new-milled lumber. Her own parents too, these
two she trusts and judges each day and swears
at them in silence.

The girl fears bears. They watch her at night
through her bedroom window. She fears Satan.
He lurks behind the shower curtain when she sits
on the toilet. She fears her father leaving
            and never returning.

The girl watches the preacher at the cold church and does
not believe what he says about hell.

She wonders if anyone she loves will die.

You Are Extraordinary

My analyst-in-training Dr. Kripke once broke the rules with me
for which I thank him. He needed analysands (*victims* I thought)
to complete his supervised hours. I had to find a place to lay
my grief. Four sessions a week. Ten dollars a session.

After months of lying on that couch using cartons of Kleenex,
revealing more than I knew could be unleashed, I had
the requisite crush on my therapist. To my 32-year-old mind
he was a perfect man. This, like everything else I dredged up
on that couch had to be explored. I was learning to speak.
I was making the developmental journey from child to adolescent
and onward to the separate being I could hope to meet
in progressive stages: myself.

The moment I remember most, the moment
I call the pinnacle of that odd time in my life:
I told this wise and beautiful man I imagined
he thought I was ordinary.
The strict rules of psychoanalysis dictating
he would make no statements
of his own opinions, giving a grunt perhaps
to let me know he had not fallen asleep.
In this case, allowing for a pause
he said "I think you are extraordinary."
He said *that*.

And because he was God I took his words
as gospel, adorning myself in the holy
raiment of these words.

I don't know if Dr. Kripke reported that deviation
to his supervisor. I will say I carried with me
his sincere statement in that moment.
I needed to hear that before I could journey onward
To the extraordinary ordinary me.

BROKEN

Don't make me say again what I don't want to believe.

If I can say the words, do not suppose I say them willingly.

The brimming world is a cadaver
and we the fleas on the dead dog keep sucking.

~

In a few hours I will have forgotten this again.

We can talk of a trip to Paris. I will say of Notre Dame

let's spend a whole day there

study High Gothic

marvel at huge columns

Broken

into smaller fluted elements.

DR. JUAN FRANCISO VACA OÑA

In my worst Spanish I answer
Dr. Juan Franciso Vaca Oña.
His shirt   crisp at this late hour
his lavender tie   true silk.
He takes my history. "Perhaps we trade
        services" he jokes hearing my work.

He listens to the threads of knots and spaces
my heart makes. He asks me about medications.
I can't remember. My fuzzy head brought me
        here tonight.

High elevation, dehydration, congenitally defective
        heart valve.

Dear heart, surely you have been
broken always.

He does not look away when I uncover
        my torso for the electrodes
a non-invasive tracing of voltage differential

Dear heart, credit must be given for
        those years without a murmur.

Now I hear the *swoosh* of surf at night
        inside me *something must be done.*

He would do the surgery himself
        quotes 25,000 dollars   *mucho menos*
        que en Los Estados Unidos.

Dr. Juan Franciso Vaca Oña,
so many thank yous   but

your lavender tie is too pale.

Give the Heart the Reverence It Deserves

Anyone investigating hearts should be advised how easily bruised hearts can be.

I am not speaking of symmetrical shapes, red usually, seen around Valentine's Day.

I refer to asymmetrical hearts that work as pumps to circulate fluid in the body.

For over a year I have circled around my heart.

This is a figure of speech indicating a wariness I feel toward this organ, my heart.

Before surgery my heart had beat continuously from the faintest fetal pulses.

My heart stopped, *was stopped,* for over an hour on January 7, 2015.

Not only do I know my heart ceased for the purpose of repair but here is something else:

Tissue from a pig now lives where the defective valve was before.

So when I say I have circled around my heart, I do not imply ingratitude.

What I ponder is how to give heart to such disruption, this invasion.

My surgeon, a Dr. Langerstrom goes into heart spaces multiple times a week.

He may collect his team in a prayer circle. I don't know.

"Surgeons think they are gods" someone said to me.

This may also account for their terrible reputation as pilots of small planes.

During transplant surgery, I have heard the heart is cut out and placed in a sterile basin.

Clarification: my heart remained in my chest cavity exposed though not beating.

A machine did the job of my own heart pump for the duration of the surgical procedure.

Last week *The New York Times Magazine* included an essay entitled "How to Hold a Heart."

The woman doctor asks nurses to wait until the heart stops beating before they take it away.

   Give The Heart The Reverence It Deserves

                          she says.

HAIKU FOR WILDFIRE

Smoking stones still smoke

charred mountains' hidden pockets

give way to green shoots.

EGYPTIAN GREEN

Each day a collection of refuse
to pick through and sort.

Tomorrow will arrive smooth
unmarked by feather holes.

tell the truth as if it is a lie

For example
dribble a color you love
Egyptian green or Moon yellow
upon a pure and fading surface
noting adequacies of his holy face.

there is a woman so full of love

She doesn't have to prove herself.
He likes her dress a little off the shoulder.

Do you think someday we will remember?
Now will seem like a long time ago.

Chicken Poem

We blamed the roosters

for the motley look of the hens

Now the roosters are all gone

     and the hens look worse than ever.

A Piece of White Cloth

(from a dream)

Someone's nightgown once

Fabricated

in a tower of sweat

Somewhere—Bangladesh?

Serves as a rag now

To wipe my oily brushes.

It hangs head down

From a peg

Arms dangling.

EDEN

On humid West Texas mornings she would rouse us
before sunrise to pull grass-burrs and even though we hated it
we loved the cool dawn and imagined this was why
God walked through Eden in the cool of the day.

The road trip in our '49 Chevy Sedan, not much of a memory—
Mother at the wheel along the same barely-paved highway
outside of Oracle in the Arizona desert, where Tom Mix
from silent movies died driving too fast and someone
put a little cross by the road to mark the curve he overshot.

I remember our mother speeding toward Tucson
hurling threats over her right shoulder at my brother
and sister in the backseat fighting and giggling,
                dodging her swats.

Up front I sit primly, the good child
in light of misbehaving siblings. This day is blistering
even with all the windows down. My bare legs stick
to the vinyl seat covers and I know I must try
to remember all of this:

Hot Wind   Roadside Crucible   Sweaty Legs

Newly-Widowed Mother   Three Half-Orphaned Children.

Horse Trek On Dartmoor

The first day's ride left us sunburned and sore.

The day after and days following cast upon us a sense

of being held in a place for which words did not exist.

Shaggy ponies, stone circles and sounds, though not

words, but shapes like blue flowers

spoke to us and for us.

Our unshod horses took whatever way they chose.

We trusted them as we did night-lavished

galaxies of white stars.

Each day's silence

lightened our heavy bodies.

Memories faded

until all members of our party

four-footed or two—

spinning spinning

toward something

large and generous.

Exquisite Copse

He didn't hear the groan.
He said "if you'd been here
you could have stopped me"
before everything
went sideways
then collapsed.

True, maybe I would
have heard the crack
of splitting post, maybe
I would have signaled
stop and he might
have stopped before
the old wisteria's
thick vines pulled down
with her the trellis
and latillas,
Support and Supported
like Samson pulling down
the temple pillars,
his long hair grown back.

The bridal wreath
too eager, more delicate
than wisteria, but those
small blossoms deceptive.
She hung on, then took
down with her the apple-
stick lathwork.

Support and Supported.

FLUFFER

I can't remember where
I heard the word *fluffer*
and had no idea what it meant.

Just a bit of ephemera captured
by my journal—it could be the woman
who turns back the bed and plumps
the pillow in a Five Star Hotel.

Then a commentator described
Lindsey Graham as *fluffer* to the ex-
President and I remembered—a term
used in porn films for the person
who keeps the man's dick up.

Rosemary

We walk out today toward the river for no reason
than the day itself and the sun warm for February.

Rosemary agile at eighty not weighed by regrets
or none she remembers. She knows she loves water.

We walk slowly only for the remarkable clarity
of unmarred blue above and our linked arms easy.

She opens her palm to show pebbles of rust, cream, black-
speckled gold she collects on our walk and polishes with spit.

Rosemary forgets why we cannot go in the river now.
She loves water, wants to fling off her clothes as she did in Greece.

She will forget the water is freezing and ask again
if we can go in. I point to the willows, tell her

when the willows have leaves, we will go in the water.
She forgets this again, forgets it ten more times
while we sit on cottonwood stumps by the edge
           of the river.

FROZEN RIVER

The frozen river white

and cracked. It stands

buckled, hard, twisted

upright, slabs like combatants

girded for battle. A silent order

and armored plates heave

concede, fall back

      motionless

as a child-commander has spoken:

      Freeze

and the river obedient

stops in its tracks.

LINDA FAIR

BACKCOUNTRY

Ice-trapped pond water belches
icicles drip/splash drip/splash drip/splash
footsteps crunch
frozen things crack: grasses,
small bones, ice dams, assumptions.

Wasn't the journey to the mind of winter,
a somewhere-else season?

You thought the subject was nature.
You read cold books, poems of rime and floe,
preparing for
something else

but the track forked
to a different
melting
a hanging glacier
hidden from view
disconnected   fall arrested
the claw marks of ancient slippage distinct.
You see the stitchings of the past strained, stained
a high cirque in unstoppable thaw.

If you had been warned
you could have made
preparations
        cancelled appointments
        turned down the thermostat

Now you unpack your distinctive voice
put away your eye for detail
set out with empty satchel, searching for form and find
honesty to be a gawky trip

and so
step
carefully
into the frozen
backcountry.

Bosque del Apache

tumble out of blue sky
frantic flurry of white
heavy bodied

black wing-tipped beings
slipstreaming onto water.
Bark   flap   primp

chatty travelers
gather for the evening.
Lightness

shimmers against leaden water,
each a moon hung
against dark sky.

Night descends.
Silence. Gray bodies
sway in water-time,

dreams hang in unison
above tucked heads.
Imagine being one

among thousands,
asleep wing to wing,
breath whistling soft

as coyote prowls the shoreline,
lifted nose, watchful.
Imagine, dawn

coming to whisper ancient words,
tumult of voices,
tornado of feathers,

to lift, as one,
your great body.

FLIGHT

Dawn shows pewter above far hills. Snow geese mutter.
Cranes untuck their heads from under dark wings,
look slowly around their lives ready to obey
what the body's deep knowing urges.
No thinking no planning no punctuation only
listening to the quiet voice of forever,
the one I have never heard
that cuts the tether from
a strangled mind—oh that I
might meld into the great
formless body,
not stay below
showered
in sound

sound of
leaving.

BEAR

I saw him only once
a huge thing
bent   black   poised
above the barbeque.

Thrilled yet frightened
I fluttered my fingers
against the window's
pane.

He turned to look my way.
I stared back stubborn,
told him with my hard eyes:
you may not eat my barbeque.

He gave me a pass, this time,
ambled round the corner of the house,
carefully crossed the strawberry patch
and disappeared into night.

This morning, I will return the shotgun
and the three bright yellow cartridges
that I borrowed from my ex-husband,
former guardian of my person,

because I have looked into the eyes of the bear.
I know him now, and being of warm heart and
little brain, I take him this day as my friend,
co-habitant of my lot

until death do us part.

MARGARITO'S PIG

I have lived in the little town of mud houses and big mountains for most of my life. But deep down, I am a mid-westerner still, a city girl. So when I looked out the window of my mud house one day and saw a huge brown pig sashaying down the dirt road, I was stunned. Now, I know nothing, absolutely nothing, about pigs. It was akin to spotting a troll under the cattle guard. I watched that pig every day for two months, taking his morning and afternoon constitutionals down and up the county road, snuffling his way from one side of the road to the other, haughty, elegant, oblivious to the more common species: the dogs, the horses, the cows, the prairie dogs, the humans. And then, one day, I didn't see Margarito's pig. Or the next day. Or the next. I never asked Margarito where the pig went. What do you *think* happens to pigs, gringa?

Summer pig   walking
your journey so sweet   so short
where do you walk now?

THE ASPARAGUS SPEAR

I came upon you   suddenly   around a corner
past the juniper tree
it was like running into a ghost
or a naked man—
yes, it was like running into a naked man in the woods

so tall you stood   unashamed   alone
how could I not notice you
your spine straight and proud   your neck
stretched into an elegant curve
like a slight bow to acknowledge my presence
yes, as if we were fated to meet

those many years when you came
to just that spot waiting for me to come
upon you though I never did
this time it happened and I was excited
and reminded that

one day I found myself standing above a fawn
curled into a bed of bluebells in the forest
where his mother had left him to sleep
while she nuzzled new grasses elsewhere
and she warned him not to move
not even his eyes
no matter what happened

and he didn't   though I came closer   and closer
to gaze upon his newness
his courage and innocence
which was not unlike yours

now I bend down
to run my fingers up the soft, slick skin of your
body, reach into my pocket and pull out
my knife, place it flat against the ground of your stem
draw it through your torso fast   painless
and before you know what has happened
my lips are around your head slipping down to your neck
and I bite slowly, tenderly
and I moan   yes   I moan at the exquisite
sweetness of your body upon my tongue.

Cherry Tomatoes

sure, things are tough at times but
at least I'm not a cherry tomato,
yet

what is it about size and accessibility
a pleasant demeanor and tenderness
that is so repellant to the Powers that be,
the Growers in all their guise(s),

who covet the deep purples and the bright
reds, the keepers and the lasters—damn
their thick skins and cocky blossom ends!

end of summer,
a touch of insanity in the garden
(human insanity, that is)
a time of excessive association with certain vegetables—

and a desire to destroy others—
     the beans the beans
will you stop growing!!!

Bringing Up the Garlic

It has been nine months
since the clove entered the ground,
since it held the soul of the garlic
through winter through freeze and heave
through darkness and through drought.
It is time to harvest the garlic.

The fork is clean.
The soil is dry.
The sun is setting.
The wheelbarrow waits.

He carefully inserts the fork 3 inches from the plant.
He presses it into the soil deep deeper then tilts and lifts.
The plant seems to fall over slightly as in a swoon.
Moving down the row tilting lifting swooning
he reaches the end

returns to the first plant and grasps the neck gently, but
firmly, pulling her from the bed. She rises clothed
in a heavy skirt of soil as if the ground were unwilling
to let her go. He grasps the mass of her skirt and twists it,
first one direction, then the other, allowing the skirt to sift
through his fingers. Creamy rootlets dangle, exposed,
particles of soil still cling. He rubs them softly
with the flat of his left hand, his right hand
covering the tender body of the bulb.

He remembers.
Garlic bulbs bruise easily.
He remembers.

I Hear the Beans Growing

in the morning

I pass a homeless man
he lurches down the highway   torn pack
clutched to shoulder-blades curled forward
bayonets planted in the top of his hat
I look away and never see his face
     instead
     I hear the beans growing
     down in my garden

in the afternoon

I walk the garden
past the dreaming potatoes in their mounded beds
past the dark green mallets of acorn squash
past the fat white onions muscled out of the soil
past the sassy whispering carrot tops
     and I'm sure I can hear the beans growing
     do you understand me?
     I hear the beans growing

in the evening

I choose from my garden who will be eaten tonight
in the cool of the late sun I peer
into the open palm of the pattypan squash
I press the taut flesh of the tomato
I touch the fur on the zucchini
     and I hear the sound of the beans growing

in the night

after I have eaten too much
I think of the man on the highway
I wonder where he is
I wonder why he limps and what he thinks
I wonder when courage will grow in my garden
     and why I can hear the beans growing

in the stillness

before dawn
a curtain of coyote-call quivers
outside my open door
it pulls at a great loneliness within
and I walk to the edge of the trees:
down in the garden
I hear the beans growing

Cuauhtemoc

The Mexican cerveza, *Dos Equis*, was introduced in 1897 to usher in the promising 20th century. A profile of Cuauhtemoc, *He Who Descends Like an Eagle,* adorns each bottle. He was hanged by Hernan Cortez in 1521 after the invasion of Tenochtitlán. Cuauhtemoc was the last Aztec emperor.

In that tight place between comfort
and the edge of outrage,
I am bound to my teachings.

How long is the alchemical journey
from ignorance
to respect
to compassion
to love ~~~

I am cramped in this anglo-saxon crib,
hunger in my belly.

How do *my* people
tear out the beating
heart and consume it?

Do we bury the past
lest it step on the present
because we are blind
to the signature of danger?

How much can we cover over?

My head twitches:
look/look away
look/look away
look/look away.

The ghost image of your culture
persists,
Indio.

August 6th, 1945

a miser I mete out a few moments to remember this day of carnage
famous cruelty rationalized as saving lives by taking lives
76 years ago and yesterday and yesterday and it will be tomorrow
we have lost our kindness and swim in unfamiliar bodies that we blame
and change as if that would fix our hearts every day death
like simple breathing sloughs poisons from our actions onto the innocent but
let's talk about me an area of which I don't yet know that I know nothing still
about the way to honesty being honesty but it won't save a child at the border
or a mother bombed in Ukraine because we have been bombed out of our
     humanity we
know nothing I know nothing I know nothing
but

     listen: I hear a birdsong a siren a gunshot the dogs want to be fed:
     half a Sierra Club cup of dry kibble one teaspoon of canned
     beef in gravy for the old one mixed quickly with a splash of
     water then

continue on with your life.

BARBARA'S RECIPE FOR ZUCCHINI BREAD IS MISSING

Forge ahead without it. You've been cooking for 55 years for God's sake.
Start with the grater.
2 zucchinis. Grate/grate/grate/grate/grate/grate/ last night I wrote a poem
about a puzzle grate/grate which sailed over on the *Queen Mary* in 1948 grate/grate.
A kind man gifted me with this grate heirloom and I am so honored grate/grate.
Dark or light bread? I choose the light today, take this as opportunity—for something—
rather than punishment for my grate/grate. This puzzle makes me think of my mother
and father when they were young, sailing back and forth to Europe with their parents
until Hitler ruined everything and the *Queen* was retrofitted into the *Grey Ghost*
grate/grate and forced to ferry the troops, shocking grate/grate and so annoying
grate to my mother. Now she's docked in Long Beach, California servicing gamblers
and whatever (the *Grey Ghost* not my mother). I have another recipe in front of me,
forgive me Barbara great baker of breads who has risen for the final time. I'm using
Canola oil. Barbara, what is a Canola? I can't think that I've ever seen one, but the
label says "neutral flavor perfect for baking". Cut down on the sugar. I heard on TV last
night that Charles Lindbergh was a eugenics believer and admired the Fuhrer and that
his baby might have been imperfect and then I turned it off. Turn on the oven to 350
degrees. Chop the nuts, add flavoring and zucchini, and beat. Does that mean beat
the mixture with my hand or an electric beater, Barbara? I should have turned the
oven on earlier! Bake in small loaf pans. These 2 belonged to my grandmother. She
was almost a regular on the *Queen Mary* but she never baked a thing in her life.
Bake for 1 hour. Cool down.

After the Oil Spill: Gulf of Mexico 2010

<u>Universe to Poet</u>

You, Poet!
>   where were you
>   when your sisters
>   cried out for help—
>   laughing gull   loon   least tern   roseate spoonbill
>   where?
>   when   glossy ibis   snowy egret   little blue heron
>   mutely called from the oily slime?
>   you didn't hear the hoarse querp of the stilt sandpiper?
>   the peep-lo of the piping plover?

>   Where is your tongue, Poet?
>   Can you go to the pain
>   can you speak   shout   gasp the truth
>   free your curdled tongue?

Poet!
>   Where were you when brother turtle—
>   loggerhead   leatherback   hawksbill   Kemps-Ridley—
>   crawled from the suffocating sea to find breath?
>   when the bluefin tuna   the whale shark   the bottle-nosed dolphin
>   drowned in their own element?

>   Why were you not there to shield
>   cormorant   brown pelican   phalarope   frigatebird?

>   Have you spoken to anyone of the dead and the dying—
>   coral reef   starfish   soft coral sea fan—
>   brown and caked
>   with death?

Where is the silky stroke of your civilized tongue
when brother osprey's great wings are spread over
oozing sand
craw in spasm   eye clouded
dying from the last supper—
he, who could never speak your language
he, who understands the unspeakable?

When did the strands that bound you to them
break?

Do you not understand
                                        Love?

DEMOCRACY'S DREAM

she rises
exhausted
another
night
picking over
        old amendments
        inalienable rights
        torn declarations

until
they flake
like dried semen
from her gown

reduced to chattel
the unwilling whore of the greedy
she thinks to end it   to abandon her citizens
scattered and troubled the exhausted executors
of failed promises

but
the dream keeps coming
every night
dawning
fresh promise

she gathers her stained skirts
and steps
again
into the light
of one
more
day

FOR JOYCE

it's always like this in April   / brutal /   winds with murder in their throats
sighted on my daffodils

I pick some this morning   / nine /   their cut stems bleed white stickiness
into the palm of my hand

I rub it between my fingers   press it to my nose   a fresh smell
curious   like blood

I think of you as I pass the rose bush you said would bring peace
and beauty to my new home

                    peace and beauty

armored limbs bulge with scabrous galls   I cannot remove them
without killing the rose

scars on my arms tell of my passion to excise the poison
I wanted you to be pleased

how could I hold peace and beauty in my home
while my country spreads gall and death

you teach me to hold   war   cruelty   beauty   peace
in the same body   mine
you teach me pain   betrayal
you teach me that I know
nothing

PRAYING MANTIS IN THE GREENHOUSE

I.
It's damn cold out
15 below and that's the gospel.

I'm wondering how it was last night
up in the pulpit of the pepper plant?
Did any of the faithful draw near
to hear the Prophet preach?

a pill bug, a cricket or two
did they attend Thee last night
seeking forgiveness and truth
—the starving and the hopeless—

and were they met with Thy all-consuming love?
O Ancient One, Child of the Oligocene,
teach me to see with Your compound eyes
teach me patience and stillness.

II.
Up here in the Ordinary, I fry an egg
and after I break my fast
I go out and look again,
seeking the miracle.

III.
The sun has risen.
I hurry to the greenhouse.
Icy air slaps my bare legs.
Inside, the smell of decomposed life.

Your bent and focused body
it's down there somewhere
in the litter   unrisen
save for the tiny egg sac.

You, who hear what I cannot
with your one ear tucked under your thigh,
tell me, tell me, what do you hear?

Tell me,
if I clasp my hands and wait
will I become a child of God?
will gifts shower upon me? or
will I become a camouflaged predator?

GORDIAN WORMS AFTER THE LONG RAIN

the universe of the daisy clump squirms
with long wriggling filaments, headless,
pale, they twine their bodies around the
flower stems. A fly and me focus on one
especially long worm, our mouths agape.
Laid out, end to end, it's got to be 24 inches.
A bumble bee weaves noisily through the
stalks but I doubt worms have ears. A red ant
sits on a daisy leaf which hosts 3 rain drops
too small to spill over. Ant contemplates the
scene before him. Big eyes swivel. If I had
weeded those tall grasses among the daisies,
would I have destroyed the high-way upon which
these worms navigated the clump? Would they
be twisting and coiling in this dance unfolding
before my eyes or would they be earthbound and
still? I confer with the fly on this matter. He knows
nothing either. Classical music plays on the radio.
Lots of strings. The worms choreograph their twists
and loops to the music.

I wonder about God.

Then Came Doubt

Hunched at the edge of the world,
Swathed in a weathered cloak, Doubt called out:
May I enter, my friends?

~~~~~

A carrion bird perched on Doubt's shoulder,
Quick-eyed eater of indecision,
One taloned foot held aloft.

~~~~~

Doubt happened upon Thomas in the town,
His Apostolic finger reaching for the bloody hole.
He took him first.

~~~~~

A huddle of old people rested by an empty well.
Sweeping the veil of denial from their leathered faces,
He said, Know me as Doubt.
And watched as their Faith
Splintered around them.

~~~~~

A church, a Bride, a Groom:
Do you promise to love and obey,
Forsaking all others 'til Doubt do you part?

~~~~~

Satiated, Doubt seated himself upon a fallen log
And watched as a rogue state murdered its people.
The bird's eyes glittered.

~~~~~

Doubt trailed his hand
Over the earth beneath him
And left his stink
On the end of time.

FALL AGAIN

Each year summer succumbs
With flurry of brittle petals
And stench of rot unseen,
Gives way, exhausted by its own
Beauty.

Each year, under the clothesline,
A parade of last minute mushrooms
Explodes from its buried bunker,
Hopeful notes from below,
Offspring of last year's spore.

Who has put wisdom in the inward parts...? Job 38:1-7, 34-41

Being Grammy

Say that you circle my wrist with your new teeth and then
look up at me
              and I
                    down at you
                          because

you don't want to take a nap.
Say that I ignore you, not wanting you to think I care about naps

                feigning
                      ennui
                         is
                            my style

Say that I read out loud to myself......poetry.......
while you pull tiny books from their shelves

turtles   dinosaurs   red trucks and the dancing hen
tumble to the floor and soon we are laughing

                laughing!
                    my love
                         for you
                            is enormous

I don't know if we did it right or not.
I don't know if you have been emotionally damaged
by my choice to read poetry instead of comforting you
but there you are in your plaid shirt face down on the blue rug at last
your arms tucked under your belly sweet green fanny poked into the air
all surrender and soft breathing and surrounded by yellow snakes
while a tall blue giraffe holds your shoes

                keeping
                    watch
                      over
                        us

FOR JACK GILBERT

Give me the crusty voice of an old poet anytime
the bleached boneness of the sound of age
dry   brittle
the minds of old men
finally come to their senses.

And then I steal their lines
the ones that catch my eye
like pretty stones wet from the sea of creation
I bring them home to save
in a poem.

I had intended to share them with you but
when I opened my heart and lay them down
I saw they had turned dull and smelly
like shells pulled from their homes
and I couldn't think why I had spent all that time lugging them around
even the silky single sounds
proscenium   plinth   spore   porcelain
could not remember why they had insisted on coming along.

And then I understood:
It was the surrender that had called to me
not the line   not the word
but the cool quiet
like a knife slicing clean
into my heart.

On Becoming a Piece of Paper

imagine
the fear of being here
of being famished for place

white sheets laying flat
the recipients of our longings   our fears

imagine how they miss standing in tall rows of green
and brown and red and grey
shoulder to shoulder snugged together
toes interwoven in darkness below
wind rustling through their leaves

imagine how sweet that was

imagine how cold and lonely
the long separation until
they regathered here
on the plastic table
sharp pointed things scratching at
their skin

can you imagine?

Inchworm Dream

The question is: can I live like the inchworm
knowing the only choice is
        to go forward
        or to die?

Can I venture out to the tender leaf edge,
torso waving, twisting, probing,
        blind
        one more time?

> *Someone is snoring*
> *a broken flute*
> *a bugle played backwards*
> *the clock ticks*
> *the dogs sleep*
> *we dream*

Eyes open, I leave inchworm behind,
folded into the back of my eyeball,
a tiny visitor caught in a snapped up window shade.

I could abandon him in the wetlands
of my eye but choose instead
to unroll him
to examine his life and mine
to explore the fragile leaf.

April Storm

1.

I do not have to save the trees
from their white-heavy load.
Born to bend, to give way
these supplicants of morning
are left bowed in prayer, though
some will not rise to greet the sun,
some will not see the sky streaking blue.

No one moves this morning
save the birds tracking the sky.
Gone the daffodils, the new apricot blossoms,
gone the stretched pink of the crabapple,
the crocus flattened forevermore.
It will be a hungry day.

But not for me, warm in my mud house
feeling alive   pampered   special
lounging barefoot admiring my toes
an observer of the vagaries of nature
out there.

2.

The sun hits the treetops.
The electricity goes out, snapped
by a heavy load dumped
from a branch too tired
to hold any longer,
and now we are all running
on our own power.

Those stealers of time—
radios
computers
telephones
televisions—
they are all gone to deep sleep
leaving me time to witness the beginning of a revolution outside.
Blocks of snow cascade down from high branches,
gathering more snow as they fall.
It is a movement,
unrest and agitation everywhere
tremblings of resistance,
shudders toward freedom.
Spines are straightening,
fingers flexing.
The junipers shiver their longing into the wind.
Infectious, this desire to throw off weight.
The woods begin to dance.
As I watch sun-patches crawl the ground,
robins flock from tree to tree,
small flunks of dropping snow bloom into
sprays and then to small explosions,

I understand that everything I need to know
today waits
out there,
freshfallen
untracked.

AFTER THE BIG WIND

You might as well know
I don't care about the wind anymore
I will not flee before
        the wind
           anymore

roots incised into ground
branches canopied
leaves pitted
        the wind
           passes through me

WHAT IF

earth decided
she'd had enough
what if she let off
a stunning explosion
or two
just to see
if anyone
was listening
and then she
let down
the way milk comes
when it's time
causing the delicate
skincrust of herself
to give way
under the weight
of us and
she crumpled
like a beautiful
blown egg
and she sucked everything
into the great lung of her
filled herself up

with the trash of us
and breathed out a sigh
of such great relief
that a moist film
covered everything
and she waited
another billion years

or so
until her insides
filled again
with the precious gems
that we stole from her
what if we gave it back
in our bones
in our salty tears
and she grew again
the mountains and the rivers
with our bodies
wouldn't that be a way to say
sorry
we hear you now
we give the shells
of ourselves
back to you

                    wouldn't it?

or

what if we heard
her explosions   heeded
her desperation
what if this terrible beauty
were the release of ancient
wrongs
what if she said
I cannot hold
your pain any longer
and we heard her
and we believed her

what if we understood
that we
like the rock   the river   the antelope
are parts
of her

what if she waited for us
what would we do
with this new
                gift
                        of time?

Gaia Mika

No Place to Root

I woke this morning hazy and a little off balance
remembering that I never felt a fondness for rhinos
until i read about their near demise
and the extraordinary human efforts to bring more rhino babies
into this world—
meaning rubber gloves up to your arm pits
reaching deep into layers of rhino innards
and hormone injections, artificial insemination and ultra sounds.
Surely an act of love.

Would I do that out of love for the whole panoply, the splendid display,
and the way it all works together?   Or did.

It's that I'm not even that open to the congregation
of aphids on the christmas cactus blossoming red in the south facing window—
they too love the sun. Nor did I feel much regret seeing the long legged spider
inadvertently sucked up by the vacuum cleaner just yesterday.

So I'm aware in a fuzzy sort of way of the vast gap
between a cherished idea and actual behavior.
Glad for the haze.

In the dream I am telling Hank we won't be able to sleep
in that uncomfortable bed for more than a few days.
My desire for comfort discordant with that innocent longing to be of use.

This doesn't, however, prevent me from entertaining that longing again
and again, from noticing that where I want to be today is in the broad boulevard
with the people, unfurling banners, laying down my own red rose
in recognition of those already lost. Crimson lines of commitment
snaking through the crowds.

Through the Internet my heart is scattered across continents.

And I wonder again, which trees will be able to walk up hill
to find a new home a few degrees cooler
and will the insects that make their home there come too,
and the birds who move up, where will they nest if their chosen grasses
can't come along, or from where will they sing without the bare branches
of their favorite tree. And what of the plants already as high as one can go.
No place to root in thin air.

WE'VE GOT THE BLUES

In the living world of mammals, amphibians and trees,
flowers, too, the rarest of colors is spectrum blue.

Bluejay feathers covered with mosaic-like beads,
cancel out every wavelength but cerulean blue.

In the painting, *My Blueness Doesn't Bother Me*,
a family's naked bodies touched by shades of blue.

The pure pleasure of smearing paint on canvass.
Listening with our eyes to smudges of blue.

Two palettes of movement along igneous cliffs.
Turquoise tipped wind waves, deep seam of blue.

Ice remembers atmospheres of pleistocene hues.
Portal to primordial memory—frozen silent blue.

Layer upon layer of distant hills, color of far away,
of where you are not and will not be, silvered blue.

Light that disperses in air, scatters in water.
Each of us, yes, you too, with our sliver of blue.

Cold Front

A journalist falls in love with the last two northern white rhinos on Earth,
in the distance they look simultaneously clumsy and graceful,

bulky but gliding—he says, at *some point we have to talk*
about rhinos as givers and receivers of love—short and plump

an old man and woman walk their yard as if contemplating
a project, he wears thick red suspenders, limps a little—even the clouds

look wind blown and have lost their shape—warblers, flycatchers
and swallows fall from the sky, already emaciated, the winds

of an untimely cold front throw them to the ground—the mountain
shy for most of the day, reveals herself icy and chilled —tires

spin on hard pack snow—as permafrost melts cold war sites, well preserved
wolves, reindeer infected with anthrax resurface—an artist

renders a depiction of a black hole about to swallow a neutron star
the collision creates ripples in space-time that pass through

Earth—a slight slip on the unseen ice—the dark settles in
when the poet isn't looking, *I just turned away for a moment* she says

missing the blue hour—time of tender transition
to another way of being, she says, *we are not the only ones*

singing—everywhere she goes the rhino moves in swirling
clouds of ox-peckers, egrets and guinea fowl—a woman creates

a storm with her body whenever it's necessary.

Maelstrom

after a painting by Hank Brusselback

we   are falling   have been
          for a while now   but hadn't felt

                              the plummeting
              air   rushing   by   upheaval
                                                until now
          our clothes   torn from us   or
              did we give them away

                          all we can feel   the falling   not hav-
              ing   had   the shock   of landing
                                                    yet
falling with   tree limbs
          empty grocery bags   banners   debris   and

          with the birds   who accompany   us   their red
              bodies   rise & dive around us   i cannot
                                  imagine
                              a world   without them

              we   are not   achingly   alone   you can   see
              the others   with us   their beauty
                          not compromised   nor yours   as you fall

          we're   close   to the other   creatures   again   the other
                  mammals   with their   big   hearts

up here   we   cannot
      see   the floods   the firestorms   the land   gobbled
              up   dumped on   bored into   can't see shrink-
          ing islands   burial sites   covered   over

i   cannot   see   the urgency
          in the faces   of the loved ones
                      is it in   the   air

                  turbulence   taking   us   is there   ease
                      in succumbing   understanding   what we have
                                                        done

but now   receiving
our guidance   from leaves

falling   like longing   not like
fleeing   are we longing   for what
we are   falling   toward

CRAVE RADIANCE

after the title of a poetry book by Elizabeth Alexander

when i flipped the book open randomly to page 51 it said,
"How ironic that we have not recognized something
that has been with us for so long."

yep, i thought, ironic. i also thought, sad

the day itself strange
filled with leftovers beauty couldn't quite touch

the smoke in the air a reminder
    your fire, my fire

the exposure to Joe's bottled up rage the night before—
i'd carried it home with me never sensing his radiance
or mine

but remembering it shine through my daughter's
    soft pink skin

the kale hangs on mostly as fragments of leaf
holding up holes

we are mostly space too though it's hard to believe when awash
    in the precariousness
    of being

my grown daughter still hasn't landed anywhere with the least bit
of softness and has very little space
for further falling
how can her sweet dreams survive this harshness

the cruelty hidden in the day to day

i struggle to keep my fear in check   will she be wrecked?

it snowed a couple of feet the day before she was born, trees
fully leafed out sagged
under its weight

i see us now walking across the field—it's her first day of school—
me with my long strides a few steps ahead

there is no illumination here
i know there is some deep fault line in my gaze
    but i have no explanations

the craving, yes, the craving for radiance, underneath it all

WORDLESS

1

Have you ever seen a greater male sage grouse
perform his courtship ritual? All I can say is—
    behold
pristine white fur-like feathers frame his face,
gold flecked eyebrows, fan of spiked tail feathers,
the undulation of his dance, chest thumping,
golden breast pouches puffing out with each in-breath.

2

The more-than-human not only enfolds
and permeates us—it exceeds us.

Think of the multitude of ways the world whispers and beckons—
inchoate, shapeless—and of the longing to decipher.

3

In Hunan Province in a rural village there once was
a woman's secret bird-worshipping society—women and birds
were interchangeable. They wrote to each other, mother
to daughter, friend to friend, in their own bird-track-like script,
a script outside the language of men. In this way the women lost
some of their shape, spilling out into the world.

4

Words want to be, desire each other. We write
from the body of amazement, from the wildness
of our eyes, the skin of our hands creating
its own script. Tears became words.

THE WOLF AND THE COW

I want you to know that, though this takes the form of a letter
it also means to be a poem, a poem about the poem we call wolf.
We don't know what they call themselves.
And you may not have heard about the Gittleson's cattle,
and that's where this poem, which is a letter, begins.

Dear Gittlesons,

I saw a photo of your cows huddled together, their thick winter coats
and big eyes, snow between their ears. I read about how three were killed
by the wolves, their bones and blood on the snow. And how, since then,
you and your family have been taking turns protecting your cows
through the night. I hear your anger about the new law, about those of us
in the cities who voted for it, how we don't care about your loss.

If you lived just a few miles north in Wyoming you could kill the wolves.
Twenty four wolves gunned down near Yellowstone just this season.

I have been feeling into your grief and anger, into the uneasiness of your cattle
especially as daybreak approaches, the wolves often arriving under cover
of fog just before dawn.

The bulky bodies of the cows, the lean and lissome wolf.
I imagine a wolf slipping out of the fog.

I've never been face to face with a wolf, but if I could, I would be
with the crowds in Yellowstone, up early, and at the right spot, to watch them.

We mammals are drawn to other mammals- to their families, their burrows,
their sense of loyalty, their practices of love.

And here I begin to have trouble finding the words
for what needs to be said. For what we might learn
about our own embeddedness if we listen to the wolves.
Perhaps you can find a better way. Your words on this subject
are needed too.

This is not about you or your cows or me and my city life, though we both
are implicated. It's not about some romantic vision of wolves—like us,
predators and a keystone species, like us, territorial,
like us, wolves nurture their young.

This is about survival, not just yours, which matters, but about our collective
need for wolves. The whole of us, the us of us, needs the wolves.

When there are enough wolves things begin to right themselves—
the elk, the deer, the cottonwoods, the creeks and you and I
come more into balance.

You probably sense the urgency underneath my words. I know,
and you must know, too, residing as you do in the mountain west,
that we cannot go forward with the way we are living.

We cannot.

COSMIC FLAME

In deep water plains on the ocean floor
lie nodules containing copper,
manganese, nickel, and cobalt
below the sunlight zone/twilight zone/midnight zone/and the abyss,
mining is about to begin in the Haldal—deepest of the deep.
They say there are mountains, deep canyons and undersea lakes
there on the ocean floor.

*

After many millions of years the sea became so crowded with Life
that the lobe finned fish crawled out onto land.
She probably didn't know if she would be able to breathe
or even what breathing was. She took the chance, though.

*

Miners will scrape
the top five inches of ocean floor,
lug up thousands of pounds of sediment,
extract the metals/ flush the rest /back into the ocean.

*

Mammals spent millions of years feeling into what it meant to be mammals,
groping toward their best forms. Cat sized horses once galloped
across north America—each of us part of an unbroken chain
of happenstance and circumstance.

*

The slurry will contain toxins/
Blankets of sediment will take lives/
Slurries will drift/will be carried by ocean currents ———

*

Not so long ago—maybe 50 million years—wolf-like carnivores waded
into the ocean, and began the very strange process of becoming
whales—marvelous beings who sing and love.

*

Microbes live
on the very nodules
miners intend to extract—
a living habitat that took millions of years to grow.

*

*A new clan of blue whales has been discovered in the Indian Ocean (the whales,
of course, already knew they existed)—this tribe's ballad bellowed slowly
is distinct from any whale song we've yet heard.*

*

Exploratory permits are being granted
in a deep water plain extending 1.7 million square miles
between Hawaii and Mexico/a zone unusually flush/with life.

*

*We now know that, with perseverance and tenderness, one of us can develop
a loving relationship with an octopus, a creature so unlike us, her strangeness
palpable. Within moments she can shift her shape, convert her color,
and she can taste what she touches.*

*

The batteries for a single electric vehicle
require 187 pounds of copper/123 pounds of nickel/
15 pounds each of manganese and cobalt/venture capital flows.

*

*We come from beings who groomed each other every day—one set of fibers
in our skin exists purely to register gentle, stroking touch—*

*

The physicist suggests—*perhaps we could see ourselves as a cosmic flame
blooming in the universe and coming to its natural end—*

Dear Brother Tom,

Been waiting for the dread to die down, for something fresh to be dished up -
something I might dream into. Finding no accomplishments to rest on.
  You've been gone long enough—maybe I can situate myself with you.
    Begin again.
    Again.

I live in a house with plenty of rooms. Houses going up all around us—
two walls stand alone across the meadow. Dogs bark. A peacock whines.
Looking out windows isn't enough. I have to go out and get into it.

The chamomile seeded itself in the cracks between the flagstone.
Drones were overhead last night. While I wander in my garden
people are crossing the Mediterranean in flimsy boats.

Lots of adjustments. You missed this phase.

The mind seems to be on the edge of one of its cliffs. Hovering.

Some days there is so much shrinkage I get folded in like a cabbage
so the soft inner leaves aren't exposed. Is it time to make room
for the others to grow? Are they growing anyway?

We are the ultimate weedy species and more and more frequently
one of us goes berserk.

Still waiting to be called out. Do you know what i mean Tom? Lured deeply
into the world without a second thought. Doubt free.

Not much coalescing here.
  The Say's phoebe built three nests in the eves. why three? Each time
    I come out on the porch she feels she has to leave.

Maybe nothing is wrong. Only some terrible realities and, some would say,
astonishing possibilities. Ants move to and fro across the courtyard.
They carry their load.

Some tips have come to me like 'stop waiting to be anointed'.
And once in a dream I was told:
'the burdened do not feel awkward, they are spinning & alive'.

The one who watches continues to worry that I won't get it right—
even making muffins can be a trial by fire. And, as I write you
the worms from the Chinese elm are crawling up the walls of the house.

I've made some decisions like, it's OK to drink coffee every day—I don't have to
save half for the next. I've given up trying to give it up for the sake of becoming
a better person. The overall project lingers on in lots of suspicious ways
and is probably behind this whole poetry endeavor, which might be why
it smells a little. We've caught 6 skunks already this season and the aroma
lingers on the door jams and window sills.

Ambition does seem to be fading—that desire to be someone—though
the other day I did try and grasp at the beauty of the day-after-the-rain-sky,

    clouds gradually opening out and breaking up,

    but sticking around all day long letting the sky show through,

And the light.

I wish you could have seen the whole day.

The clouds, I think, are why i came here.

THE GRASS WAITING

rain thundering down, trees drenched tomatoes drenched kale
and carrots drenched, squash bugs drowned and mud,
actual mud like long ago new mexico springs, splattered
on zucchini leaves big enough to hide behind—could the ponderosa,
so dry they should be dead, feel revived like I do tonight? and
the new moon partially veiled by a thin layer of cloud left over
from the downpour. and the dry crumbled thoughts loosening.
and the pollo frito playing louisiana music at the adobe bar,
the drummer dripping with sweat and smiles, a new orleans divinity
of delight, the lead guitar listening to his own sweet notes, eyes
closed. and the rain softening the edges of troubled minds.
and the grass no longer waiting.

I AWOKE WONDERING

what i would write
in the circle
on the large
black tablet
set by my bed
remembering
the flood
of conversation
with strangers
at the edge
of sleep
and when i asked
myself honestly
whether
in this moment
i truly believe
that i
will die
some day
i have to
admit that
despite
the very strong
evidence
i feel
as if
i'm here
and am always
going to be
here
and maybe
that is why
a day can
disappear
without

being
relished
which would
be a sin
if i believed
in sin
and even
after finding
a full grown
broccoli plant
had fallen over
sometime
during the night
i still wasn't
convinced-
was its own
magnificence
too much
to bear?
i crave
the world
so much
i'm willing
to step
over
my dread
just to be
in it
and even when
i'm stripped
bare
of purpose
i can
sit with
the wild earth
and learn

how to listen
and i am
still
wondering
if i will
ever get
to see
the ocotillo
bloom-
how much
is enough
rain to
inspire
those
tiny red
blossoms?

Could You Be Clear With Me

Were you there with me
curled in the crook of the willow tree

looking out through lace of leaf and branch,
even then trying to gather myself

to listen.

Or hidden in nests of tall straw
colored grass when the animals
were still alive in me

learning delicacy and skitishness
through a spindle-legged presence

wildness through the arching of her neck
and the pounding of her hooves.

Was that you also
in the awkwardness?

Did you tell me what I'm here for

unheard through the din
or never clearly translated,
listening interrupted by mounting desire

so that even now I can't be sure.

Yes you were there when the whales
came close. When I ached to see them
rise and received their blessing.

And you are in the reciprocities
and great swirls of love.

But are you in the faces of strangers
who huddle close as I fall asleep,
sometimes muttering instructions or advice?

Is it the labor of garden love
you want from me? The amazement

as garlic bulbs are pulled from the earth
the fury at the surge of flea beetles,
the fury at the seige of Gaza.

NAKED WINDSHIELDS

Before
I read about
the insect
apocalypse
I had noticed
the windshield
not smattered
with smushed bugs
remembered
childhood trips
the three of us
in the backseat
me day-dreaming myself
into the cultural stories
designed
for teenage girls
the hood of the green plymouth and the windshield layered
with bug bodies   wings   yellow blood
it turns out
insects
have many
sub brains
in different parts
of their bodies
so some parts
can operate
on their own
the antennae has its own brain   the mouth   the eyes   each leg
so if needed bug legs can keep working without the help
of the central brain

since we define
intelligence
in comparison
to our own
we miss
a great deal
of intelligent
behavior
I suspect
we need bugs
more than they
need us
it has only been
quite recently
I have been able
to include insects
in my basket
of care
and now
I am asking
why leave anyone
out

KIN
(with)
ancient arches
abrupt cliff walls
absences layered
bacterium our bedrock and
bones
canyons
cut through by wren's
descending song
deepened by diminishment
everywhere eating and eaten
entangled exertion
egret elephant
furrows baked in with
fear—ferocious fear—and forgetting
gesturing toward grief
grasses murmur and bow in congregation
 (seed themselves elsewhere)
gazania gloriosa goat head
humming haunted hub of relationship
invisible innards exposed
 (back to bones) and earth
inhabitants can be
jubilant
joshua tree many armed
joshua tree
keening
kinship knowledge held by
land itself how to
learn this
listen to
laughing goats, lovage and lavender
meander in teaming
meadow's multiplicity
need nourishment not to be
numb never just
one of us

one within the
other
prayers under fallen logs
piles of prayers in tangled branches
pulse of peptides become proteins
plutonium pellets
quicker than the eye
queering ourselves into atmospheric
rivers resonant (with the body, through the body)
reciprocities shaped by
reciprocities
seeds and soil seep of beauty
songs move life along
stones roll
tarnished tides plasticized our
tattered skin our teeth our flesh our
thirst
undone
viruses spill into us
water & wind whisperers of kin
we can all break can we
wait
yearning
while the moon slides back to
zero

Thomas Frances Simon Aquinas
(My Dad)

He squints into the sun, flannel lined jean jacket, old plaid wool tam askew,
some sense of tired satisfaction. He's had a morning of prying
abalone from underwater ledges, a hobby taken up in his 50s,
their muscular foot needing to be tenderized before he fries them up
in a bread crumb batter.

Some Sunday mornings he made politsinki, Slavic crepes filled
with homemade pear jam, or cottage cheese for Mom
who didn't want it sweet. His unabashed and abiding love
for our Mom.

But it wasn't the politsinki, I'm sure of that.

A great appetite fueled his days—things taken up whole
heartedly—cultivation of prize camellias, wood sculptures
fashioned from tree roots and drift wood, rock-hounding
through the desert and mountain west in the old white dodge van,
homemade halloween costumes.

Curiosity's blessings delivered him from Catholicism's constraints,
brought him to experimental art, erotic literature.

Was it his fondness for lamb chops and roast beef, for edam,
sharp cheddar and smelly limburger that left him short of breath
that fall in Colorado? Was it the occasional flurries of rage, anxiety's
long reach? Or was it the recklessness of his love for life—dumpster
diving in a parking lot for some old weather beaten wood
that just might come in handy?
His last act of creative pursuit.

How many love poems unwritten.

Anniversary Poem

Do you remember
silent walks along
the old railroad grade
arms entwined
slow steps synchronized
us bursting
with quiet delight

held by the secret blessing
of the meditation master.

Years wrapped around us
we kept on walking, roamed
neighborhoods after dark
laughed after dark have
come this far.

Your wild multi dimensional mind
dreams voluptuous
ceilings, undulating roof lines
rearranges rooms in morning
reverie of shifting shapes.

Wrapped in your father's
checkered shirt
devotional deities hover
help you
smear paint
faithful to your muse
ardor in each
brush stroke
each truth told.

Your daily praise songs
for simple conversation,
fellow workers, big bold
sky, fresh night air
pour out
take the edge off
injustices piling up.

Weathered but not worn
made porous by longings'
ceaselessness
outer layers easily pierced to
hearts unfolding
you are tender to the touch.

I'm still singing your song
you and I still held in that
original blessing.

Think of Trying to Explain Beauty

Think of arctic ice melt
walrus, without summer
ice, wedged
uneasy
massive body
against massive
body
a hundred thousand
crushed on a small strip
of land near the sea.
Think of it,
then drag your old body
outside to the shimmering
leaves to be smitten
by the intricate interior
of the outrageously orange
tulip- maybe not what the bee sees
but beauty enough
to draw you in.
And the biologists and ornithologists
ask, *could large feathers*
have evolved simply
to be beautiful
and your soul,
little as you know it,
quivers with confidence
as you think of king penguins,
orange and black beaks,
dolphining as if soaring through
Antarctic waves running
a gauntlet of sea lions to reach
their young, recognizing the cry
of their own amidst thousands.

Go ahead, think of
our evolutionary backslide
our propensity for caging
for clamping down
craving to punish
what we cannot love.
Then close the screen,
let those old feet
relearn barefoot
in the grass
on the warm flagstone.
Go out after
high desert rain
run among the scattering
red-orange paintbrush.
Find your favorite spot for brooding
and listen,
the evening grosbeaks singing still,
you pondering
beauty
and the evolution of a consciousness
that cannot thrive without it.

EXTINCTION

A poet once said "'real' poems do not 'really' require words."*
I've sensed this myself—
        that actions themselves can be poems.
I'd like to give an example though, of course, by describing this action
in words, I can't help but move the action into the realm of poetry.

Here is the account.**

Two men agreed to spend 4 days and 3 nights backpacking in a cornfield
in Grundy County, Iowa.

Now you may not think this sounds like bravery or like poem material
or like love, but you might change your mind, Iowa being a state
that devotes 90% of its land to the practice of mostly mono-cultural
agriculture, this particular field containing 600 acres of pesticide-glazed
Dupont corn engineered to contain the genes of an insect killing worm
and cellular resistance to herbicides.

Maybe you are starting to sense the danger of their project.

These two men entered the Owen's family corn field one July day
in the midst of a meteorological anomaly; 900 record highs
across the country that week. The men were encased in a heat dome—
a 2000 mile wide cell of very hot air sitting over
the North American continent. It was close to 130 degrees Fahrenheit.
Bandanas covering their faces, sweat soaked and scurfy
        with corn pollen they walked
        heads bent and hands clasped behind their backs
        through row after orderly row
        stalks 8 feet high
        rows shoulder width apart
        leaf blades genetically modified to allow in maximum sunlight
        each modification part of an effort to grow more corn on less land.
The heat took their breath away.
The leaves closed in around them.
They suffocated the impulse to flee.

By this time you could be wondering why they would continue this journey

They walked through the rows of corn looking for what else, if anything,
might be alive in this once vast expanse of tall grass prairie—switch grass,
blue joint, side oats, brome—that supported 300 species of plants,
60 species of mammals, 300 species of birds and over a thousand insects,
and where now mostly corn and soy grow.
An ancient mosaic of interacting habitats long gone.
Elk and bison long gone.

They wanted to know, *What's left?*.
>The two men asked farmer Owens how long the soil in these parts
>could hold up.
>He said, "You don't want to know".
>Mrs. Owens pulled them aside, told them,
>"I've been doing this kind of farming most of my life.
>I don't think what we're doing now is good for the earth."

In a drainage on an edge of the corn rows they set up their tents,
found clouds of grasshoppers kept out of the corn by the atrazine,
found white tail deer moving through,
saw a delta winged katydid clutching a grass stem,
saw a black stink beetle trudging along.
They were besieged by mosquitoes.

I hope, at this point you might be considering your own poems
that do not really require words.

They walked, crouched, sometimes lay on their backs in the rows.
The heat took their breath away.
Looking up through the stalks they could barely see
a washed out half-white sky.
The leaves were sharp and cut through their clothes and skin.
They walked breathing in atrazine and anhydrous ammonia
in order to find out what else might still be living.
They found one tiny wax cap mushroom at the base of a corn stalk,
found a cobweb spider and a crane fly caught in its web,
found a red mite and an ant, found

a crab spider
a thumb sized toad
some deer tracks amidst the corn
a sphinx moth
and they heard one bird move above them.
On the third day they fled.

* Layli Longsoldier
** For the full story please read chapter 6, Species Vanish,
    in *Apocalyptic Planet* by Craig Childs

A Name is Needed for a Living Creature to be Formally Assessed for Extinction Risk

It could have been me who discovered you in the Ecuadorian rain forest.
Me making rain soaked sightings of you as froglet, you as tadpole,
scribbling my observations in waterproof notebooks,
taking measurements of the width of your toe webbing,
the distance between your nostrils.
All of this necessary before the naming,
before we could know you,
grass-green and yellow tree frog,
as Mashpi.
Without a name
you could have disappeared
without our knowing,
without our grief.
Many have.
We try to find them
and name them
before they're gone
in order
to save them
from ourselves.

An Undoing

There will be an undoing which will guide the poem.
It begins when she doesn't meet her "soul mate,"
she doesn't throw her lot in with that disturbance.
The mesmerizing mystification of snow never settles into her soma
so she doesn't lose the house in the sweet old tree-lined neighborhood.
Sun streams in through the east windows of her cozy bedroom.
She doesn't lose the research job at the clinic.
Me and my terror never drive all night to the hospital in Albuquerque;
I don't drag thru days witnessing her anguish, the nurses' disgust.
Those erratic years—their toll never taken.
Her psyche not shaken by a night spent in jail.
For months she doesn't sleep in her car,
doesn't sleep in a different neighborhood each night.
No need to wonder where she will pee in the morning, where she will clean up.
The methadone remains in the bottle, a form of restoration that does not heal.
She breathes deeply, sleeps on her side or her back,
debilitating worry doesn't reverberate through her days.
The swelling in her legs has softened—she walks without pain,
strolls around the lake in the morning,
watches redwing blackbirds swoop in and out of the reeds.
She is at ease.

My Rare Friend

We talked on the phone, he in the house
where you no longer are. How we can
be there and then be gone.

All the things you touched, your love
in the hallways and the stairwell,
your stashed stuff spilling

out of drawers and cupboards. Projects
in midair. Are they still waiting for you
to come back down the stairs?

Months ago when you first told me, sobbing
together on the phone, you wondered
if you had been too good, too well

behaved, worked too hard. The remnants
of a habit, and who could know, really.
Nothing to be fixed or repaired.

You were a great burst of kindness, steady
like a long walk.

Gaps of time between us evaporated
with ease—never lost
to each other, maybe even now.

Lucky to have visited you those days
in late April not long after
you took the fall, your once smooth hair

shocked wiry, eyes vibrant like a bolt
of blue lightening, that same wry
smile, slightly impish, twinkling. We sat

on the upper deck, trees holding us,
chatting & napping. You were reading
novels; no longer reading about death.

Acceptance had taken root in you along
side stubbornness and the hope for a miracle.
And you knew how to pray. The grace

that arrived graced us all before she
took you with her. You're not here
for the glowing white night, for the world
glimpsed through the architecture of trees.
Still and all, you're here in me.

MY BLUENESS DOESN'T BOTHER ME

In response to a painting of the same name by Hank Brusselback

Beneath the surface
of everyday loving
here on the inside of life
the inexplicable breath
small gestures of naked
tenderness
our bedrock
each of us with our touch
of blue
reminders of the risk
of being in a body
round soft bellies
of the young
and in the corner
older boys
the only ones clothed
already sensing
danger
beginning to play
with uncertainty and threat
to try on courage
with the colors they wear
to keep
fear's secrets
and nakedness
apprehending
even now
how life wants
to change us

WATER HELD BY ROCK

The last message I received on the rocks was to follow
the water lines. Violet sky shimmered in rain puddles scattered
across slick rock. We dipped red handkerchiefs, dribbled the coolness
down our necks, rested skin to skin on a shaded stone slab.

Rocks speak the language of water rounded and sliced through.
Water murmurs, whispers of feeling, layered flows
shape ledges and basins, seep through fissures and fractures,
find their way to the root. Wheat, corn and soy move across the globe
carrying the memory of water.

In the dream we were wading waist deep in a glistening pond,
canyon walls rising around us in beauty.

Rock and water share a discourse of upheaval—
cliffs soar toward clouds of swollen rivers,
flows of people take to water, ghost boats haunt the sea.
Cool pools of water continuously bathe nuclear reactors.

Suddenly I knew there was something beneath the glassy surface
not to be touched. I called out to the others.

Perhaps life came into being in the warmth of a tidal pool: water held by rock.
We gather deep in the canyon near the confluence
of two endangered rivers, all of us in white we
wear our sorrow on the outside. We bring offerings.
We sing to her from the banks. Sometimes we shine.

SAUCY GOLD

The squash, forced to leave the vine before they were ready, are in an incubator of sorts, sitting in the October sun until their skins turn tan while their stems, looking like tiny hats, harden and dry. Two of them lean toward a third where they stand upright yet relaxed on a stone bench—one that will hold the heat even as the sun leaves, or should I say the earth turns? And do you ever feel it, the earth turning that is, do you ever feel our spinning, circling home, like the folk in Antarctica who listen to the ice cracking, groaning and shifting. I've longed to be that sensitive, though not too sensitive, and therein lies the bind- the path of pleasing others is one of ultimate failure. I am pretty sure the squash are not on that path though they will surely please us in the form of squash soup with chili and mint, and the color they will offer up to the barrenness of winter—warm, rich, saucy gold.

Have I said anything about their conviviality—their apparent conversation on the stone bench, watching the black cat go by without a nod to them, as they look out over the garden perhaps with nostalgia for the days when the vines were flowering and they were attached, perhaps wishing they had been allowed to come to maturity in the proper way, worrying about how their goodness might be compromised by the loss, the cut off, yet recognizing that they have it pretty good right now, sitting in the sun all day, coming into the warm house at night to cuddle in their boxes.

They will soon be wrapped in newspaper, separated from their skin-to-skin contact and placed in the dark cold of the shed. And they haven't seen the headlines. Once they're separated from the vine are they still capable of sensing my distress, as plants can do, the distress being present most days as I try to get my bearings in a world going mad. The real predators are on the inside now, always hungry for more, and it's not squash they crave.

YOU CAN WATCH THE BREAKDOWN OF ORDER
AS LIFE UNFURLS IN FRONT OF YOU

1

Five elephants pass slowly through a car dealership,
blind to traffic ordinances they cross
multi-lane highways,
squash chickens,
poke their trunks through the window
of a nursing home.

2

Most mornings the robin returns
throwing herself over and over
against the window
of the tiny workshop
in the backyard,
perhaps hoping to arrive
in some imagined paradise.
Speaking softly, I say,
sweetheart you are hurting yourself with no hope
of getting what you want.

3

When a turtle has eaten
a discarded plastic food container
her stomach signals her brain
that she is full. She makes
no effort to eat
and starves to death.

4

The Chinese cabbage flowered
before its leaves could begin
to curl inward to form a head.

5

When asked what they want to be when they grow up
millions of young people say,
famous.

6

Destination unknown, the elephants, who are hundreds of miles
from their nature preserve home, are trailed
by officers, emergency vehicles, and drones.
With wonder and intoxicated delight
millions of Chinese citizens track the elephant's progress.

7

We walked from fire to fire this past year, some of us seeking
as much distraction as possible, fear and grief
dancing in a tangled web of love.

8

Steam rising from sun-touched surfaces
after a heavy rain.

9

On the ridge, spare white branches of long-ago-burned trees
rise above aspen and jack pine of the young forest,
branches awkwardly bent toward our solar system's star,
others twisted toward the earth,
like sentinels transmitting prayers
from earth to sun
and sun to earth.

Acknowledgments

We are grateful for mentors and sibling poets who have inspired us, nourished us, offered up lines and words, and encouraged us to show up on the page. Much appreciation to Judith and Kate who wrote with us at the kitchen table, and to Sawnie whose creative teaching buoyed so much of this work.

ABOUT THE AUTHORS

Gaia, Linda, Judith

JUDITH BUFFALOE

Judith lives along the Rio Grande in Northern New Mexico. She is self-taught as an artist, professionally trained as a family therapist and mediator. She writes poems to observe the world and catch bits of this world in words. She describes her work as feeding and being fed by a stream of dreams, images and silence inspired by the naked beauty of New Mexico.

LINDA FAIR

Linda's poetry, essays, and literary reviews have appeared in *Turning Wheel, The Horsefly, Drinking from the Stream,* and *HOWL Magazine*. A dedicated gardener and environmentalist, she finds guidance and inspiration from the natural world— the world that speaks in other tongues. She lives in Taos, New Mexico.

GAIA MIKA

Gaia Mika lives in Boulder, CO where she frequently falls into wonder tending her vegetable and pollinator gardens. As a poet she aspires to engage fully with the beauty and brokenness of the world. Currently she is working on some local climate justice projects, and for years she worked at the University of Colorado as a psychologist, teacher and consultant.

Made in the USA
Middletown, DE
09 April 2023

28415151R00070